Mental
Pull-ups

D0907994

by Karen Boscaljon
Edited by Alice B. Acheson

Sta-Kris, Inc.
Marshalltown, Iowa

Printed and bound in the Republic of Korea

Printed by Dong-A Publishing and Printing Co., Ltd.

Published by Sta-Kris, Inc.,
P.O. Box 1131, Marshalltown, Iowa 50158

ISBN 1-882835-33-6

Introduction

Health. We tend to take it for granted until it deteriorates. Today we know there is power in our thoughts, emotions, values and beliefs – enough power to dramatically change the state of our health. Health is about learning how to develop a delicate balance of the body, mind, soul and emotions. It takes time, energy and commitment to develop health. Challenge yourself to a higher standard of health starting today with some mental pull-ups.

To Alice: What a healthy team we are! You found all of my misplaced modifiers and I found the seven glasses of water a day you were missing.

Mental Pull-ups

1• Strive for a healthy balance in life. Look for the people, places and influences that support a healthy body and mind.

2• The ten two-letter words that have the power to change your life, "If it is to be, it is up to me". Put it into practice.

3• No one needs to lose more than ten pounds, although some of us need to lose ten pounds six or seven times.

Mental Pull-ups

4•   Check with your doctor before beginning *any* exercise program.

5•   Exercise speeds the digestive process allowing fewer calories to be absorbed.

6•   On your next doctor's visit carry a list of symptoms and questions listed in order of your concern. You will save time and have more answers.

Mental Pull-ups

7• General health guidelines recommend drinking eight eight-ounce glasses of water a day. Not only will it make you feel "fuller" it will provide the kidneys and other organs the fluid these need to operate at optimum capacity. Other liquids will not achieve this goal.

8• Challenge your own excuses; it frees up other people's time.

9• Every ten pounds lost is another clothing size to count down.

Mental Pull-ups

10• No one will accidentally wake up at 5:30 a.m., jog three miles, commune with God and spend quality time with the family before work. Set goals.

11• Self-acceptance is critical to success. Rarely will we work hard to help someone we don't like. If the person we don't like is us, we won't work to reach our goals. Success begins with liking yourself.

12• Exercise *decreases* hunger and *increases* energy.

Mental Pull-ups

13• Your value as a person is *not* determined by your weight.

14• Food that literally takes seconds to eat can cause grief for weeks!

15• Everyone is motivated. It's not a question of *if* you are motivated, it is a question of *what* you are motivated to do.

16• Focus on what you really can change. Accept what you can't. Don't continue confusing the two.

Mental Pull-ups

17• Health, wholeness and holy are all derived from the same Greek root word. Think about the connection.

18• One pound of muscle burns 45 calories a day, one pound of fat burns 2 calories a day. Building muscle is the most effective way to lose and maintain a lower weight.

19• The result of stress can be felt by the body more than a year after a crisis is resolved.

Mental Pull-ups

20•
Contemplate the difference
between hunger and appetite.
When you eat, hunger is satisfied.
When you are feeding an
appetite, it wants more. Appetite
is never totally satisfied.

Mental Pull-ups

21•   Eat your food slowly and concentrate on how it tastes.

22•   For those who believe they absolutely cannot stick to a program of healthy eating, ask yourself how many days you could follow a healthy eating program if someone paid you $1000.00 a day. If you believe that you could follow a healthy eating program for $1000.00 a day, the question is not one of ability, it's one of commitment.

Mental Pull-ups

23•   Saying you will start exercising tomorrow is a copout. Don't try, do it! Not tomorrow, today!

24•   You may need to teach someone how to hold you accountable. Accountability is 1.) *not* a lecture, 2.) *not* taking food away from others and/or 3.) *not* making guilt-oriented statements. Accountability *is* asking others if they met *their* goals.

25•   People change when they are ready to change, not when we are ready for them to change.

Mental Pull-ups

26• Only 1/100% of the population can meet society's ideal standard of height and weight.

27• Rather than assuming that what you are feeling is hunger, ask yourself if you are hungry, bored, tired, or anxious. Learn to identify what you are feeling without eating your way through your emotions.

28• If you lose weight faster than two pounds a week, you are losing muscle you need. For best results lose a pound or two a week.

Mental Pull-ups

29•   Healthy eating can directly control or prevent: high blood pressure, high cholesterol, indigestion, ulcers, constipation, diabetes, obesity and some dental problems.

30•   Lose enough weight to get rid of the hangy-over parts.

31•   Visualize putting the "unhealthy" you in a box, sealing it with tape and mentally placing it on the top shelf of a closet.

Mental Pull-ups

32• There is a moment when it is just as easy to eat a food as it is to not eat it. Recognize that moment and make a healthy decision.

33• Americans consume over ten times the amount of sodium they need. Limit your sodium consumption to between 1,100 to 3,000 milligrams a day.

34• Your optimum weight is one where you have the most energy and feel good physically.

Mental
Pull-ups

35•   Skipping meals is a sure way to weigh more. This one bad habit may be the single biggest problem some people have that slows down their metabolism.

36•   Simple carbohydrates should be avoided. These foods have been refined to remove much of the fiber, vitamins and minerals, leaving mainly sugar. White flour, white rice, refined sugar, bakery goods and sugar coated cereals are examples of foods to avoid.

Mental Pull-ups

37• The scale is the poorest way to measure your success.

38• You may not be eating too much food at all, just the wrong type. Challenge yourself to learn about proper nutrition.

39• You will probably not lose weight every week. Focus your goals on the *process* of what you need to do, not the *result*.

40• Choices. Choices. Choices. You have them.

Mental Pull-ups

41• Chocolate is a complex food. It contains 400 distinct chemicals and all of them are fattening!

42• The body produces 80% of its own cholesterol; 20% comes from dietary sources. Although genetics may be the cause, the amount of french fries and cheeseburgers we consume are within our control.

43• Canola oil is the healthiest vegetable oil choice. (It is, however, still 100% fat).

Mental Pull-ups

44• Triglycerides are blood fats influenced by diet, exercise and genetic factors. Levels between 100-150 are acceptable, but higher rates may increase risk of cardiovascular disease.

45• Our biggest setback may be in realizing we are our own worst friend. We buy foods that set us up for disaster, tell ourself we will never be successful and violate our own goals.

Mental Pull-ups

46• The body does not always lose weight and inches in the same week. The week you do not lose weight may be the week you lose inches.

47• Find a healthy role model. What do they do that you are not doing?

48• Holidays are all year long. Don't wait until "after the holidays" to eat right. As soon as one is over the stores have the seasonal candy out for the next one. The holiday cycle is never over.

Mental
Pull-ups

49•
There are always three versions
of what you eat: What you are
going to eat, what you ate and
what you said you ate.

Mental Pull-ups

50• If you fall, get up and try again. And again. And again. And again.

51• Most people are more aware of the weather and the time than they are of the stress in their own body.

52• Never be fooled by short-term apathy. The fleeting thoughts that say you don't care about your weight or health will quickly be replaced with remorse.

Mental Pull-ups

53• Walking is a great cardiovascular exercise. If you jogged an eight and one-half minute mile, you would only burn 26 more calories than if you walked a 12 minute mile.

54• It is entirely possible to eat small amounts of high fat food, exercise and gain weight.

55• Try writing down everything you eat for a week. Calculate the fats and calories. Look for success and error.

Mental Pull-ups

56• Look for fun measures of weight-loss success like moving your belt buckle over another notch, pants getting longer, buying a smaller size, shoes or watch bands that have become too big. The best measure of success is feeling more contented with yourself as you are.

57• Great low fat dessert: Mix 1 can of lemon pie filling with the powder from any one-step angel food cake mix. Bake on a jelly-roll pan for 25 minutes at 350 degrees. One piece is 0 grams of fat.

Mental Pull-ups

58• The goal of controlling unhealthy eating is to see how far apart you can make it from the last unhealthy eating episode. No one will eat only healthy foods forever, every time. Work to minimize the frequency of the destructive episodes.

59• Women who learned to play sports at an early age were found to have an advantage in business. The experience taught teamwork, cooperation and risk taking. Is it time to enroll your children in a sport?

Mental Pull-ups

60• If you are determined to eat high fat foods, don't ask others to eat them with you.

61• Isn't it weird how we dread losing weight and look forward to it all at once?

62• Do you want to lose weight or are you just wishing? Wishing won't allow you to reach your goals. If you think about all the things you have really WANTED, you have probably gotten them. Do you really want to lose weight or are you wishing?

Mental Pull-ups

63• You may need to fake it until you can make it. In other words, think of yourself as healthy and making healthy choices even if you are not there yet. Healthy thinking will lead to healthy behavior.

64• What would happen if the government taxed fat and poor health? Isn't incentive a wonderful thing?

65• Friendships can increase stress. Build friendships with healthy people.

Mental
Pull-ups

66• We may need to figure out what's eating us rather than what we are eating to find the source of our problems.

67• Begin a simple exercise program with a walk around the block. Work up to exercising three to five times a week for at least 30 minutes at a rate that makes you sweat but still allows you to carry on a conversation.

68• Commitment or Compromise? Only you can choose which philosophy you will follow.

Mental
Pull-ups

69• The first 20 minutes of exercise will benefit the heart and organs and burn calories; exercise beyond the first 20 minutes will burn stored fat.

70• A low fat diet is endorsed by the American Cancer Society, The American Dietetic Association, The Heart Association, The American Diabetic Association. Make sure any eating program you follow is credible.

71• Stop the process of low self-esteem that becomes high self-hate.

Mental Pull-ups

72•   Don't assume that low-fat means low calories. Some manufacturers increase the amount of sugar to mask the loss of fat.

73•   Adhering to a healthy eating plan means monitoring the amount of fat, the amount of sugar, the amount of fiber and the amount of sodium, in that order. Specific health problems may alter that sequence.

74•   Is your focus failure or success?

Mental Pull-ups

75• Many people feel the need to splurge when eating in a restaurant. Determine how often you eat out. If you find you eat out several times a week, you cannot enjoy the luxury of "splurging" each time you eat out.

76• It takes 20 minutes for the stomach and the brain to know you are full. It is easy to consume over 2000 calories before you even know your hunger has passed.

77• Value health not thinness.

Mental
Pull-ups

78• Don't be fooled by an innocent salad. Without monitoring exactly what is in the salad, you can accumulate a whopping 2000 calories and 80 grams of fat.

79• Burnout is stress left unchecked. It is a condition of physical and mental exhaustion that occurs because of continuous emotional pressure for prolonged periods of time. Those most susceptible are in professions that require them to deal with people on a regular basis.

Mental Pull-ups

80• If the buttons won't button and the zippers won't zip, isn't it time to stop making excuses?

81• Learn to take responsibility for what you do well. Focus on your positive qualities. List them on paper. Work to improve the things you already do well rather than agonizing over the things you see as deficiencies.

82• Avoid stopping and starting during exercise. You lose the maximum benefit of exercise and put additional strain on the heart.

Mental Pull-ups

83• Look at specific packaging when determining the value of a food. A bagel can be anywhere from zero to five grams of fat, anywhere from 160 to 600 calories — even without cream cheese.

84• If you are in poor physical condition, or elderly, wait two or three hours after eating before exercising.

85• Get buck-naked with your thinking. Be honest with you about you.

Mental Pull-ups

86• Isn't it a wonderful thing that after two days of eating correctly you have a new respect for yourself? You feel thinner whether you have lost any weight or not — because what you have lost is apathy and mental anguish.

87• Many health problems are thought to have a genetic link. Whether the basis of the problem is genetic or self-inflicted, the solution is the same: responsible action and behavior.

Mental Pull-ups

88• Do a kitchen make over. Clean out the bags of junk food and make a commitment not to bring them back in.

89• There is no such thing as being fat and happy.

90• An exercise companion is a good way to get yourself motivated. It's difficult to explain to your exercise partner that you just didn't feel like getting up at 6:00 a.m.

Mental
Pull-ups

91•   Make your life easier. There are many new computer software programs available that do everything from calculating fat grams, to developing personal menus and to printing out your grocery list.

92•   Be assertive when you dine out. You are paying to be served what you want. Ask how items are made, whether yours can be cooked without butter or oil and if your vegetables can be steamed.

Mental Pull-ups

93• Self-acceptance is a decision about how YOU see yourself.

94• Select exercise options that fit your personality and you will be likely to commit yourself to a program on a long term basis. Are you competitive? Do you prefer exercising indoors or outdoors? Would you prefer exercising alone or with others? How much time do you have? Do you like to sweat? In other words, find an exercise you will enjoy!

Mental Pull-ups

95•
Chronic dieters tend to *overestimate* their physical activity and *underestimate* what they eat by as much as 50%.

Mental Pull-ups

96• You can reduce the amount of sugar in a recipe by 1/3 without affecting the texture or taste by much.

97• Learn to revise favorite recipes to healthy recipes.

98• Trim all visible fat from meat before cooking.

99• One gram of fat is nine calories. One gram of carbohydrate is four calories. Choosing to move to a low-fat eating program automatically reduces your caloric intake by more than 50%.

Mental Pull-ups

100• Exercise! Exercise! Exercise!

101• You already know the result of quitting, but you don't know what will happen if you persevere!

102• Much of depression can be attributed to too little sleep, too little exercise, too much sugar and too much alcohol.

103• If everything is a priority to you, nothing is a priority.

Mental Pull-ups

104• Take charge of your feelings rather than letting your feelings control you.

105• Shrimp is high in cholesterol and very low in fat. Eat in moderation foods high in cholesterol.

106• Limit yourself to one weigh-in a week. Allowing someone else to weigh you provides some accountability. If you are weighing yourself more often begin to do it away from home.

Mental Pull-ups

107• Nothing you can eat will taste as good as thin feels.

108• Remove the salt and sugar from the table. If you are not ready to give up the salt shaker, try filling it with seven parts pepper, one part salt.

109• Change your definition of "good food". Good food is a grilled chicken breast, steamed broccoli and whole wheat bread.

Mental Pull-ups

110• If a person restricts calories or fat below recommended levels, the body will go into a conservation mode and weight loss will slow down or stop all together.

111• The higher the fat content, the longer it takes for the food to pass through the digestive tract allowing additional fat to be absorbed.

112• Success is the difference between doing something almost right and doing it exactly right.

Mental Pull-ups

113• Make a baked potato one of your favorite foods. It is low in calories and fat and a great fast food choice. After four minutes in the microwave it can be topped with low-fat cottage cheese, applesauce, fat-free sour cream, vegetables with low-fat cheese, low-fat gravy, or salsa. Be creative!

114• Excess fat inhibits oxygen intake — breathing is harder, causing less oxygen to be available to burn excess fat.

Mental Pull-ups

115• You know you are at goal weight when you can pull your queen-size panty hose up over your head and tie a knot on top.

116• The next time you feel like eating, write down specifically what you are feeling. Some research suggests that we eat what we feel. Journaling may help identify and vent the emotions.

117• Isn't it strange that no one ever seems to binge on brussels sprouts?

Mental Pull-ups

118• It is possible to have a healthy cholesterol level and a high triglyceride level.

119• Park your car in the space farthest from the door.

120• Substitute an equal amount of applesauce for oil in breads and muffins.

121• Update your body image. It can take a year or longer to adjust to changes in body size. A fat mind cannot see a thin body.

Mental Pull-ups

122• The body fluctuates as much as two to three pounds throughout the day. It does not mean you have gained weight.

123• You never again need to weigh as much as you do right now.

124• Know a fat disguise when you see one. They will commonly be listed as: shortening, oil, lard, butter, margarine, mayonnaise, lecithin, glycosides, tallow or suet.

Mental Pull-ups

125• Mentally correct a behavior following an incident. In your mind, replay the scene and visualize yourself making the right choice.

126• Burnout results in fatigue, depression and mental exhaustion.

127• Take the stairs rather than the elevator whenever possible.

128• Increase the amount of spices and extracts in your cooking and you will not notice the loss of fat.

Mental Pull-ups

129• Although alcohol is no-fat or low-fat, it alters the metabolism and slows or eliminates weight loss.

130• We stumble because our bodies have limitations, our minds have limitations and we have limited faith in ourselves.

131• One way to raise your HDL or high density lipoproteins (good cholesterol) is exercise.

132• As your craving for spiritual things increases, you find your need for food decreases.

Mental Pull-ups

133• Eat your calories rather than drinking them. You will feel much more satisfied eating an orange rather than drinking a few ounces of orange juice.

134• Is food your best friend?

135• Look for improvement, not miracles.

136• As the body ages, muscles become stiffer and less elastic. Work on flexibility to reduce your chance for injury. Warm-up and cool-down before and after exercise also increases flexibility.

Mental Pull-ups

137• Sugar offers the body no nutritional value although it contains no fat. Minimize the amount you consume. If a product has more than 16 grams of sugar you are consuming four teaspoons of sugar your body does not need.

138• Four basic food groups that cause problems: l.) Food that's not healthy. 2.) Food that is good for you but is eventually thrown out. 3.) Food the dog won't even eat. 4.) Food you wish you had thrown out and hadn't eaten.

Mental Pull-ups

139• Women in thin-oriented societies have twice the depression rate as women not in thin-oriented societies. Africa here I come.

140• If you are rebelling because losing weight is something you HAVE to do rather than WANT to do, you'll never make it happen.

141• Compare yourself to you. Are you better than you were a year ago?

Mental Pull-ups

142• Buy a low-fat cookbook with pictures.

143• Five grams of fat is equal to one teaspoon of fat. A cookie with 12 grams of fat contains 2.5 teaspoons of fat.

144• A three-ounce serving of meat is about the size of a deck of playing cards.

145• Commitment means hanging in there through the easy and the difficult times.

Mental Pull-ups

146•

List 15 things you like about yourself. Don't stop the assignment until you reach 15 items. Read and reread the list until you can take ownership of what you like about you!

Mental Pull-ups

147• Self-discipline is a critical link between who we are and who we want to be.

148• After cutting calories in half an obese person who has poor muscle tone and fails to exercise can still weigh the same and maybe even more.

149• We will "like" whatever food we get used to.

150• Rinsing meat does not affect its cholesterol level.

151• Ask for support. Teach others how to help you.

Mental Pull-ups

152• Worry is negative goal-setting. Train your mind to think positively!

153• Bite the hand that feeds you.

154• Turn in your membership to the clean plate club.

155• Food is not our reward; diets are not our punishment. It is actually quite the opposite that is true.

156• Don't premeditate a diet disaster.

Mental Pull-ups

157• A dream come true — some foods are so low in calories and fat that you burn calories and lose weight eating them: apples, green beans, beets, carrots, spinach, mushrooms, lemons, eggplant, grapefruit, cauliflower and onions.

158• Realize that the desire to eat something is a suggestion from your mind, not a command that you must follow.

159• Put leftovers away immediately and avoid the temptation to finish them off.

Mental Pull-ups

160• If you have a bathroom scale at home and find yourself weighing once to several times a day, try gluing the scale to the bathroom ceiling. Now feel free to weigh as often as you like.

161• Try mustard instead of mayonnaise.

162• Even if you reach perfection at something, you will never be able to maintain perfection. Learn when to let go.

Mental Pull-ups

163• Do you focus on catastrophe? Determine what is the best thing that can happen and the worst thing that can happen. Then realize that the future is probably somewhere between the two.

164• Worrying and being overwhelmed mentally by the work we need to do takes more time than the actual work. Stop the mental turmoil; just get the work done!

165• A positive attitude is a philosophy of life, it's not the way people are born.

Mental Pull-ups

166• Try rating your hunger on a scale of 1-10. If 10 is that bloated sick feeling of eating too much and one is starving, realize that you will really be most comfortable eating to level five or six.

167• Find a low fat substitute for the food you are craving.

168• Realize you always have choices. You can choose to eat or not eat an unhealthy food or to wait and have it later. Waiting often will reduce or eliminate desire for the food.

Mental
Pull-ups

169• Measure yourself every two to three months. You may have lost inches of fat but show minimal amounts of weight loss.

170• Fat stored in the abdomen increases the risk of heart disease. To know if you need to reduce fat, measure the smallest part of your waist and the widest part of the buttocks. Divide the waist measurement by the hip measurement. If the waist to hip ratio is .8 or above for women, or .95 or above for men, it places you at risk. Check with your doctor.

Mental Pull-ups

171•

It is possible to eat over 1500 calories in less than 12 minutes. When determining how much you are eating, focus on the amount of fat and calories rather than the time spent.

Mental Pull-ups

172• Not all weight is equal. A pound of fat, a pound of bones and a pound of muscle all weigh the same, but take up different amounts of space. Muscle takes up five times less room than fat.

173• Frequent weighing will only interfere with your goals. If your weight is up you are likely to be so discouraged you'll just eat anyway; if your weight is down it can be reason to reward yourself in a counter-productive way.

Mental Pull-ups

174• Look for ways to increase your level of daily activity. Increasing daily activity is not meant to replace exercise but rather to supplement it.

175• Don't feel you need to do everything you are asked to do. Select the invitations and requests that mean something to you.

176• Leave your TV off for one entire week and see how much time you have to do the things you don't have time to do.

Mental Pull-ups

177• Don't substitute one vice for another.

178• If you are of the opinion that five pounds is not very much weight to gain or lose, tape 20 sticks of butter on your body and look in the mirror.

179• Learn to manage your energy. Give 100% of who you are to what you are doing. If you are exercising, give 100% of yourself. If you are playing, play 100%. If you are relaxing, give 100% of yourself to it.

Mental Pull-ups

180• Figure out what your biggest "time vacuum" is and look for ways to monitor or eliminate it.

181• If you are a worrier, set a specific time to worry. Allow yourself to worry between 1:00 and 1:10 every day. If you begin to worry after 1:10, tell yourself you must wait until tomorrow at 1:00 to worry.

182• Avoid shopping on an empty stomach. Avoid shopping with an empty head. Eat first and carry a list.

Mental Pull-ups

183• Ask the waiter to bring out only one-half of the serving while dining out and ask for the leftovers to be brought out with the check. Or you may find it works as well to ask for a doggie bag and split the meal BEFORE you being to eat.

184• Airlines cater to low-fat or low-calorie meals as long as you give several days notice.

185. The world is not "all or nothing" in regards to health. The healthiest thing to do is to keep working in spite of slip-ups.

Mental Pull-ups

186• Fill out your menu a week in advance,
then follow it.

187• There is a slim chance of losing weight and
keeping it off without both exercise and a healthy
diet.

188• Spice up your life! If you reduce or remove sugar
and fat, you will be disappointed with the result
unless you add spices.

Mental Pull-ups

189• You can achieve perfection but never maintain it. Give yourself some slack.

190• If you find most of your calories are consumed during the pre-meal activities, try using your crock pot more often to minimize the time spent in the kitchen. Make sure you are using low-fat recipes.

191• Lose some fat in your head. It may be time to change your thinking on some things.

Mental Pull-ups

192• Play with numbers— determine when you have lost 10% of your goal, 20%, 50% and so on.

193• Be knowledgeable about eating disorders. It helps to set boundaries on your own behavior.

194• Clothing that leaves those lovely red indentions around the waist should be viewed as hazardous to your health.

Mental Pull-ups

195•
Discipline is the critical link
between thinking and behavior.

Mental Pull-ups

196• Alcohol not only contains calories, it lowers your resistance to foods that you would have easily passed up if you had not been drinking.

197• Dietary fat should be less than 30% of our total daily caloric intake.

198• Make a list of the things that stress you out. Decide what you can eliminate or change.

199• Attitude is everything.

Mental Pull-ups

200• Running around with your head cut off and climbing the walls doesn't count as exercise.

201• The average office chair rolls eight miles a year. Does your office chair get more exercise rolling across the floor than you do?

202• Exercise builds enkephalins and endorphins that suppress pain and produce the body's own natural anti-depressant.

Mental Pull-ups

203• After an illness, resume activity at 30% of your normal level. If you normally walk three miles, begin at one mile until you feel better.

204• An old English proverb: "Don't dig your grave with your knife and fork."

205• Think productive, not destructive.

206• Don't eat to prevent hunger. Eat because you are hungry.

Mental Pull-ups

207• Good shoes may be the most important part of
your workout. Don't compromise by wearing
shoes without proper support. If you walk for
exercise, you may need to replace your walking
shoes every 100 to 300 miles.

208• Your *philosophy* is nothing if it isn't your
autobiography. You have to put into practice what
you believe. All the knowledge in the world will
not make you healthy unless you apply the
knowledge.

Mental Pull-ups

209• Health is something that is never completely achieved. You never reach it. You keep working for improvement.

210• If you find yourself eating every time you walk into the house, try coming home through a different door, or making the kitchen off limits the first hour you are home.

211• Most people forget what they really ate during the day. They remember what they should have eaten during the day and forget the rest. Write it down.

Mental Pull-ups

212• Turkey is a great food. With different spices you can make it taste like anything you want.

213• If we are too concerned about where we want to go, we may forget to plan how to get there and never reach our destination.

214• Losing weight is fun! Look for a bone you've never seen before!

Mental Pull-ups

215• The body takes five to ten days to acclimate itself to different weather patterns. You may need to adjust your outdoor exercise to account for these changes.

216• Realize that food cravings are a normal part of life.

217• Excessive dieting can slow down the metabolism by 20% for over a year once proper eating habits have been established.

Mental Pull-ups

218• Focus on long-term goals. Short-term thinking depletes us of energy.

219• Look for a personal pattern of weight loss. You may only lose two or three weeks out of every month in spite of healthy eating. Don't interpret this as meaning that the program isn't working for you.

Mental Pull-ups

220• If you are changing on the outside, it doesn't guarantee you are changing on the inside. Many people are disappointed when reaching goal weight that nothing has really changed at all. Challenge yourself to work on *internal* health.

221• Make sure you take at least five minutes to warm up and five minutes to cool down when you exercise.

222• Caffeine increases stress.

Mental Pull-ups

223• Dress comfortably when exercising.

224• Most large-boned people are quite surprised to find they are not after losing weight.

225• If you've gone to the hard work of exercising, don't spoil it by eating something high in fat or calories.

226• Your clothing is like the wrapping on a package. It doesn't change what is on the inside, but it will affect people's reaction to you.

Mental Pull-ups

227•

You cannot control how quickly you lose weight. You can control how closely you follow a healthy plan of eating.

Mental Pull-ups

228• Check your self-perception. Try sketching your size on newsprint. Then lay on top of the drawing and have someone else draw around your actual body in a different color of marker. Compare the two drawings.

229• Limit yourself to eating in just one place at home. If you don't, you will get "food cues" from multiple places in your home.

Mental Pull-ups

230• You may find the TV is responsible for many of your cravings. Count how many food commercials are shown during your viewing time. Watching TV is a low metabolic activity, and those commercials can easily stimulate your appetite.

231• Cholesterol is a calorie-free waxy substance. The body needs some cholesterol. Too much, however, clogs the arteries.

232• What message are you giving others about yourself?

Mental Pull-ups

233• The truth is we make ourselves happy or sad.
Never rely on others to make you happy, never
blame others for making you sad.

234• It is possible to eat and do all the right things in
any given week and still gain weight. Don't
become discouraged!

235• Eat something green today.

236• Exercise. It will make every organ in your body
hum, rattle and roll.

Mental
Pull-ups

237• Compete only with yourself.

238• The scale cannot measure your success, look at the scale as merely a method of accountability.

239• Burnout is "I" centered and leaves its victims with a loss of hope. It sounds like this: "I" can't cope, "I" am exhausted, "I" can't get everything done, "I" am overwhelmed. Find one positive in your life and begin moving on.

Mental Pull-ups

240• Stress is caused by two primary sources: small hassles and major life events. Focus on controlling what you can and removing as many of the small hassles when and where possible.

241• It's been said that diets are for people who are "thick and tired" of it. How tired of thick are you?

242• Exercise technique is important. Doing sit-ups incorrectly may result in the waist increasing in size rather than decreasing, or you may end up straining your back muscles.

Mental Pull-ups

243• Reward yourself with something other than food.

244• If you eliminate only 200 calories a day, you will lose 20 pounds in one year.

245• When appetite is eating you, try waiting 20 minutes before you give in to the temptation.

246• Everyone worries about weight plateaus, but a bigger problem is an attitude plateau — when our desire to eat is as strong as our desire to lose weight.

Mental Pull-ups

247• Say goodby to a food you love that always gets you into trouble. Be prepared to grieve.

248• If you were thin today what would you do differently? Go do it anyway.

249• Get rid of the clothes that are too big for you. If there is nothing in the closet to grow into, you won't.

250• Lose enough weight to play ball and go swimming with your children or grandchildren.

Mental Pull-ups

251• If you would rather stay home and eat, work to improve your social life.

252• It is easier to turn down food because it is unhealthy rather than because it is fattening.

253• Decreasing your intake by as little as one slice of bread every day for a year will amount to a weight loss of ten pounds or more.

Mental
Pull-ups

254•

Don't feel you need to be good at an exercise to do it. As long as you are working regularly it doesn't matter whether you are as fast, as smooth, or as skilled as others that are exercising.

Mental Pull-ups

255• Problems stay the same, but WE can change.

256• What you feed, grows. That is true of the body, the mind and the soul. It is true of positive and negative information.

257• Fall in love with a vegetable.

258• They say healthy is a state of mind. Do you need to relocate?

Mental Pull-ups

259• Breakfast jump-starts the metabolism — don't leave home without it.

260• Every child deserves the opportunity to grow up with a healthy body and mind.

261• React positively to a negative situation. That is empowerment!

262• The good intention of being healthy is simply not enough.

Mental Pull-ups

263• You are in trouble when your idea of exercise is eating dessert.

264• Habits become our identity.

265• Build friendships with people that like to exercise.

266• Never go hungry to an eating occasion.

267• Treat yourself to new underwear.

268• Four words to remove from your vocabulary: "It's a bad day."

Mental Pull-ups

269• Focus on small and manageable changes in your life.

270• Don't bake food to make someone happy; hug them instead.

271• Cholesterol and fats are not the same thing. Only animal fats contain cholesterol.

272• A product that is cholesterol free may be very high in fat. Some oils are cholesterol free, but 100% fat.

Mental Pull-ups

273• Saturated fats raise blood cholesterol levels. Saturated fats are fats that are solid at room temperature and often are stored at room temperature.

274• Unsaturated fats are liquid at room temperature.

275• Following exercise, the metabolism is elevated by 25% for 12-15 hours and remains elevated for an additional 10% above resting rate for as long as 48 hours.

Mental Pull-ups

276• What options have you given yourself? If eating foods high in calories and fat are options, you will eat them.

277• Focus on how you feel, not on how you look.

278• Healthy eating is not self-renovation, but a commitment to a new lifestyle.

279• Make some mental muscle. Stretch your mind and take a class or read a book.

Mental Pull-ups

280• Wouldn't it be great to walk into the 5-7-9 clothing store without having to add all those numbers together to get your size?

281• Look at yourself more objectively. It is okay that you have imperfections. In that way we are all the same.

282• Become what you admire.

283• Ask yourself if a disturbing message is fact or opinion. A fact can be proven, an opinion cannot.

Mental Pull-ups

284• If you have a day where you have made poor food selections, begin immediately to minimize the damage. Eat some vegetables or drink eight glasses of water. You may not finish out the day the way you wanted, but it will never become as bad as it could.

285• No good diets begin tomorrow. Start yours today.

286• Learn to say "no". Now learn to say it without guilt.

Mental Pull-ups

287• If you have eaten healthy for even one day, you have proven to yourself you can do it. Anything else is just an excuse.

288• There are many reasons why people gain weight. Make sure you are not dealing with a medical problem while attempting to determine why you have gained weight.

289• Children should not be limited on their fat and cholesterol level unless directed by a doctor to do so.

Mental Pull-ups

290• We need to make our weight the "smallest" part of who we are. Decrease the amount of time you dwell on how heavy you are, how much you dislike yourself, how much you hate your size, or how much you weigh. Instead, think about health.

291• Never put someone else on a healthy eating plan because it makes you feel better. Health must be determined individually.

292• Fats supply energy to the body and help in the absorption of vitamins A, D, E, and K.

Mental
Pull-ups

293• Are you hooked on adrenaline? If you go through life on a go, go, go schedule; stop, stop, stop and think about what you are doing to yourself.

294• Slow down your entire pace. Eat slower, drive slower, talk slower, work slower.

295• Rinsing ground beef for several minutes under hot water after cooking will reduce the fat content by as much as one half.

Mental Pull-ups

296• If the size of your clothing bothers you, cut the size out of your clothes. Focus on your health, not your size.

297• Keep a record of binge eating. Figure out the time of day, level of stress, what initiated the binge, how long it lasted and how you stopped it. Learn from the experience.

298• Figure out how many times a week you eat out. Are you making healthy eating choices when you do?

Mental Pull-ups

299• What have you taught others about yourself? Have you taught them that if they put a high fat food in front of you that you will eat it? If you eat high fat foods placed in front of you, don't expect others to stop providing you those food choices.

300• When eating at fast food places, ask if you can exchange the soft drink in the kids' meals for milk, and do the same for yourself.

301• Read the labels on foods in the grocery store before you put the items in your cart.

Mental Pull-ups

302• Learn to read the stress signals from your body: pain, irritability, sleeplessness, or feelings of fatigue.

303• Give up the Superwoman and Superman goal. Even if "you have it all," it's just a matter of time before you will want to give it all back.

304• Weight maintenance is a range between three pounds below your optimum weight and three pounds above. Healthy people fluctuate without guilt or worry.

Mental Pull-ups

305• *Never* try to remove all fat from your diet. Fat is an essential component that fuels the body. Not only does it supply energy, it increases the metabolism and gives elasticity to the skin. Fat also helps in the absorption of critical vitamins the body needs to be healthy.

306• A repetitive exercise burns 40% more fat during a workout than a non-repetitive exercise. Repetitive exercise includes walking, swimming, jogging, cycling (not motor).

Mental Pull-ups

307• Finish the job you've started. Sometimes we run out of reasons to reach our goals because we've lost sight of where we are going. Few of us would wear a shirt half-sewn, eat a casserole half-cooked, or ride in an airplane half-assembled. Finish the job.

308• Winning is the result of hard work and perseverance.

Mental Pull-ups

309• Most Americans eat less than half of the daily fiber necessary. Work up slowly to increase your fiber intake to 25-30 grams a day. Fiber is the one best way to avoid cancer of the colon, helps in elimination, provides a feeling of being full and improves general health.

310• Do you mistakenly determine your value as a person based on what the scale says?

311• Respect yourself for who you are, not what you eat.

Mental
Pull-ups

312•
There is tremendous power in
accountability. Find someone
who will hold you accountable.

Mental Pull-ups

313• Build bridges between where you are and where you want to be. Building a bridge is accomplished by making small and deliberate changes.

314• Manage your stress load by scheduling high stress projects during low stress periods of time.

315• There are many kinds of pain; physical, financial, emotional and spiritual. Expect some.

316• Forget diets forever. Make a commitment to a healthy eating plan for a lifetime.

Mental
Pull-ups

317• Strength training is exercise that builds muscle. When exercise time is divided to include both weight training and a cardiovascular work out, studies show the workout will result in as much as 2-1/2 times as much fat reduction, although there is no difference in weight loss.

318• The average Thanksgiving meal is 6,123 calories and 367 grams of fat per person.

Mental Pull-ups

319• If you have leftovers from Thanksgiving for supper, you may have doubled your consumption of calories and fat.

320• Change occurs best when you accept where you are rather than where you want to be.

321• Repeat the following: No. No. No. No. No. No. No. Now that you've practiced, use the word where you need it the most.

Mental Pull-ups

322• Sugar has no nutritional value. Americans get 35% of their daily caloric intake from sugar, and eat an average of 160 pounds of sugar per year.

323• Complex carbohydrates are superior to simple carbohydrates because they contain starch, vitamins, fiber and minerals in addition to sugar. Fruits, vegetables, whole grain breads and cereals, rice and beans are good examples of complex carbohydrates. Simple carbohydrates contain more sugar and other highly refined ingredients.

Mental Pull-ups

324• Accept a compliment and say, "Thank you." Stop there! Don't minimize what someone is trying to communicate to you. Really listen to the compliment and replay it over in your mind.

325• Don't buy into the media's misconception of beauty. Dandruff and seborrhea do not make you a person of lesser value, they just make you itch more.

326• The menstrual cycle burns up to 300 calories a day. Maybe PMS isn't so bad after all.

Mental Pull-ups

327• Stress originates from three primary places; our thinking, our environment and our body.

328• If you know what you are going to eat without opening the menu, it will prevent you from being enticed by something you see on the menu.

329• A four-letter word — with five letters — for the health conscious: fried.

Mental Pull-ups

330• Changing what you eat will effect: mood, tension, anxiety, headaches, fatigue and insomnia. This can work against your health or for your benefit.

331• When changing your diet, you will notice the effects in a matter of days, but it will take over three months to establish healthy eating habits as a matter of lifestyle.

332• Make sure you are getting a variety of foods in your diet.

Mental Pull-ups

333• You need 50-60 nutrients to maintain a healthy body. This includes vitamins, minerals, amino acids, fatty acids and energy. Some foods contain multiple nutrients. Some foods contain no nutritional value. Be picky!

334• High levels of body fat and cholesterol increase the risk of heart attack and stroke.

335• The best "dieters" are not those that eat the least. Many people find that when they eat correctly, they eat more than they were previously eating.

Mental Pull-ups

336• Try drinking a glass of water before each meal and one directly following.

337• The average person has 45 miles of nerves in their body. When you feel someone has just stepped on your last nerve, make it a policy not to respond to the last situation. It is rarely the one that caused the stress and will not solve the problem.

338• Begin to take care of yourself. Begin today.

Mental Pull-ups

339•
Drinking water is the best way to lose water weight — it's a safe and effective diuretic.

Mental Pull-ups

340• When the kidneys do not have enough fluid to operate they rely on the liver for help. Consequently, the liver cannot get to its job of metabolizing stored fat. More fat will remain stored and will minimize weight loss.

341• If the colon does not get enough water, constipation is the end result.

Mental Pull-ups

342• Make a list and prioritize your next day's work before you leave at night. When you arrive at work the next morning begin immediately on the first task on your list. You will save a considerable amount of time.

343• Become a success story.

344• The question is: will you respect yourself in the morning?

Mental Pull-ups

345• Most restaurant servings are actually two to three servings of food.

346• Don't bother trying to lose weight for a wedding or reunion. Do it for you, because it's what you want to have happen in your life.

347• The absence of stress is death. Stress is not bad, but it does need to be moderated.

Mental Pull-ups

348• If you could have done it alone, you would have already reached your health goals. Get help.

349• Get an attitude check-up.

350• Find a strategy to drink eight glasses of water each day. Some of you are gluggers, some sippers and some of you are simply suckers. Glug the water, sip it all day or suck through a straw; eight glasses of water is eight glasses of water, no matter how you chose to drink it.

Mental Pull-ups

351• Old habits will never completely die. Resurrecting an old habit is a choice.

352• Invest time daily in the body, the mind and the soul.

353• Eat cake at your son's or daughter's wedding.

354• Some of us try to purchase health. We join health clubs and purchase exercise equipment to make us healthy. Health is something we do, not purchase.

Mental Pull-ups

355• If you have a negative thought that invades your thoughts, try wearing a rubber band around your wrist and snapping it each time the thought returns.

356• Foods that are high in magnesium are spinach, oatmeal, baked potato, shredded wheat and tofu.

357• If you view food as the only way to celebrate, you will constantly feel deprived.

Mental Pull-ups

358• When was the last time you complimented yourself?

359• Why is it that at the height of our stress the phone rings, someone is at the door and the kids try to flush the cat down the toilet?

360• Develop some defensive strategies to prevent weight gain and some offensive strategies to lose weight.

Mental Pull-ups

361• If you can come to grips with the worst thing that can happen, you have a healthy mindset. Then continue to hope for the best.

362• If you tell yourself you can't, you're right — no matter what the subject.

363• Taking on one more little thing, never is one more little thing. Almost without exception it will require more time and energy than you predicted.

Mental Pull-ups

364• Realize you are vulnerable for a short time following stress and change. Monitor your choices carefully during this time.

365• Alcohol is high in calories and low in nutrients. It depletes the body of vitamins you need to cope with stress.

366• Love and discipline are functions of each other. Disciplining yourself requires loving yourself.

Mental
Pull-ups

367•
It's been said that motivation is when your dreams put on their work clothes. Maybe it's time to get to work.

Mental Pull-ups

368• The body, the mind and the soul are intricately connected. A change in any one of these areas affects the others. The combination is what determines our health.

369• Stress, you can't leave home without it. Funny, you can't stay home without it either!

Mental Pull-ups

370• Focus on ability, not experience. Your experience may indicate failure, yet if you have reached your health goal even one time, you've proven you have the ability. It's not experience but ability that determines success.

371• What do you think about while you exercise? Research shows people who use mental time constructively while exercising will feel more invigorated and positive about exercise.

Mental Pull-ups

372• When exercising you should be working hard enough to be slightly short of breath, but not gasping for air.

373• Self-sabotage can occur when you buy something, bake something, serve something, or store something.

Mental Pull-ups

374• Gaining weight is a sign of relapse. So is anger, pulling away from your support group, obsession with food, and rationalizing when you are eating something that you should not.

375• Look in the mirror and determine to make peace with the person that looks back at you. If you share the mirror, make peace with your partner also.

Mental Pull-ups

376• Live with an attitude of forgiveness, not for what it will do for the other person, not because the other one deserves to be forgiven, but because it will do wonders for you.

377• Improve your integrity. Make the record of your work something that no one questions.

378• Treat others in a way that will build their self-esteem. In the process, you feel better about yourself.

Mental Pull-ups

379• When you select your friends, focus on their character before their personality.

380• Incorporate daily stress relievers, preferably of the non-chocolate variety.

381• Take the amount of time you spend thinking about food — when and how you would get that food — and use that time to decide when and where you will exercise.

Mental Pull-ups

382• Keep a stress diary. Does a physical symptom accompany the stress? Your body may be trying to tell you something.

383• Move beyond your past. Get professional help if you find it impossible to do so by yourself.

384• Differentiate between reasons and excuses for not living a healthy lifestyle.

Mental Pull-ups

385• "Dieting" did not make you thin in the past and will not make you thin in the future. Keep focused on healthy eating, not dieting.

386• Consider yourself a professional health manager. Evaluate your eating and exercise behaviors and recommend a course of action.

Mental Pull-ups

387•

Drop the "should have's." It is too late to go back and change what you should have done.

Mental Pull-ups

388• It is a lot easier to fly high when your landing gear isn't so heavy.

389• Develop a hobby that has nothing to do with food.

390• Find a safe place to fail or succeed.

391• Lose weight, not hope.

392• When relocating, move closer to family — nuclear families thrive on the support of the extended family.

Mental Pull-ups

393• Much of our stress is self-imposed. Often stress comes from faulty thinking and perceptions.

394• You know what will happen if you give up, but you don't really know what will happen if you swallow your pride and keep working in spite of disappointment or failure.

395• Never confuse failure on a project with failure as a person.

Mental Pull-ups

396• Look for everyday things that make you laugh, like the newspaper ad that read: "For sale, dog, eats anything, especially fond of small children."

397• Avoid getting hungry, tired, angry and lonely all at once.

398• Conflicting information confuses many people about which offers greater value: exercise and then eat, or eat and then exercise. Of greater importance is what will fit into your lifestyle on a long term basis.

Mental Pull-ups

399• What we *do* dictates our priorities; they are not really priorities if we *only* think or talk about them.

400• Leave for work early and notice how much lower your stress level is.

401• When working on a long-term goal, break down the goal into small chunks. Give yourself deadlines for each small chunk and record on a calendar when they must be completed.

Mental Pull-ups

402• Don't work to know just your deficiencies. Analyze what you do well and why.

403• A quarter-pound cheeseburger has the same number of fat grams as three grilled chicken sandwiches.

404• Choose to be a survivor, not a victim.

405• Work to be actively attractive.

Mental Pull-ups

406• Our metabolic rate is the body's rate of heat production and is measured in calories burned per hour.

407• It will always seem like the right choice to eat unhealthy food for a few fleeting minutes.

408• Work health into the rhythm of your everyday life.

409• Even an eagle needs a flight plan to get off the ground.

Mental Pull-ups

410• Don't rob yourself of what you could look like.

411• Attitudes are contagious. Catch a good one.

412• Always maintain some sense of independence.

413• When you are eating correctly, you don't need to be hungry.

414• Get a Ph.D. in yourself. Know your limits, know your stresses, and know your pleasures.

Mental Pull-ups

415• Set measurable and specific goals. After you've set them, ask yourself if you can make the goals more measurable and specific. Continue to refine the goals until you CANNOT make the goals more measurable or specific.

416• Who deserves to lose weight more that you? Who has tried harder or wants to be at goal weight more than you? Cooperate with your dreams.

Mental Pull-ups

417• Weakness is strength out of balance. Can you reverse this trend with one weakness you currently have?

418• Exercise that benefits the heart needs to work your cardiovascular system to 80% of its capacity.

419• Slow, gradual change will probably be more beneficial than a complete one-stop self-renovation program where you change everything you don't like all at once.

Mental
Pull-ups

420•
Exercise only on days that begin
with "T": Tuesday, Thursday,
Today, Tomorrow, Taturday and
Tunday.

Mental Pull-ups

421• Don't mistake motion for action. You need to do the right things to be healthy, not just be busy and moving.

422• It may take an entire year for your mind to recognize the amount of weight you have lost once you reach goal. It also takes a year for the mind to realize how much weight has been gained in a year.

Mental Pull-ups

423• Rarely do people get what they deserve any week they weigh themselves. Sometimes the loss or gain doesn't show until the next week.

424• Analyze the number of fat grams and calories in your daily food choices. It's not occasional splurges that create health problems, it's daily splurges. Find them and make alternate choices.

425• Most fat is in our head, not our body. Lose some *thoughts* that cause you to gain weight.

Mental Pull-ups

426• It has been said that failure is a dress rehearsal for success. Welcome failure as much as success. Although more painful, failure is the better teacher.

427• Health math: calories that are never counted tend to multiply and divide all over the body.

428• Change begins with honesty. Be honest with yourself about your health: what you do, what you drink, what you eat.

Mental Pull-ups

429• A carbohydrate calorie and a fat calorie are not metabolized the same. That sheds light on why the 1000-calorie-per-day diet doesn't work when you eat two 500-calorie pieces of pecan pie.

430• A lifestyle change means establishing new traditions.

431• Saying we have no time to exercise is simply an excuse. Everyone has the same amount of time. What we choose to do is a matter of priority, not time.

Mental Pull-ups

432• Remember that there are always people around who can help. The question is, will you let them?

433• Side stitches are a warning sign of dehydration. To prevent this irritation, drink eight ounces of water 20 minutes prior to exercising. Drink approximately every 20 minutes during exercise to keep hydrated. Lack of water will prevent you from exercising to your potential.

434• Focus on what your body *needs*, not what it *wants*.

Mental Pull-ups

435• Figure out what you believe about life, death and eternity. Then test out what you believe to be true by investing faith, time and energy into that belief. See if what you believe provides strength. Belief alone does not make something true.

436• Avoid health products that aren't: coffee enemas, a fork that lights up when there is too much food on it, weight loss tablets made from pond scum and a whipping device that promises to end your battle with cellulite.

Mental
Pull-ups

437• Don't be discouraged if people notice weight loss in your face. It's not that the face is the only place that weight loss is evident, it is rather a reflection of where people look first and most often.

438• Cereals are great low fat nutritional snacks. Or are they? When 25 cereals were tested for nutritional value, 16 of the 25 had more nutritional value in the box than in the cereal itself.

439• Laughter and tears are both medicinal.

Mental Pull-ups

440•
Never, ever give up. Always have
a mental pull-up ready.

About the Author

Karen Boscaljon is a human resource developer and a powerful motivational speaker whose dynamic interactive presentations are sprinkled with humor and insight. For the last twelve years, Karen has been a business consultant, promoting wellness to groups and individuals through seminars and counseling.

A learner as well, Karen has a undergraduate degree in psychology and recently completed her M.S. in education. She lives in Marshalltown, Iowa, with her husband and four children.

Do You Have a Success Story?

We all thrive on them! Other people's successes give us the courage to keep working toward our goal when attainment seems impossible or at least very far away.

What keeps you going when you feel like quitting? If you would like to share a short paragraph about your success, please write me at:

Karen Boscaljon
P.O. Box 1131
Marshalltown, IA 50158